# A Winter Wonderland

Leslie Arnott
Illustrated by Joan Waites

The train came to a stop in
Quebec City.
"This looks like a very cold place,"
Ramona said.

"I'll hail a cab to take us
to our room," said Papa.

Ramona just said, "Brrr!"

"Quebec City has the biggest
Winter Carnival in the world!"
said Mama.
"The three of us will have so much fun."

"You will see, Ramona," said Papa.
"It's like a winter wonderland."

Ramona just said "Brrr!" again.

By the next day, the sun was out.
Now Ramona didn't care about
the cold.

First she had fun watching a race.
Dogs pulled sleds right down the
main street!

Then Ramona watched people make
animals and other things from snow.

That night there was a parade.

A big snowman waved at Ramona.

She waved right back.

The next morning, Ramona ate some
thin pancakes.

"I love French food!" she told Mama
and Papa when she was done.

Then Papa and Ramona raced down
a hill together.
At the end of the race, they shouted,
"It's a tie!"

That night Ramona went skating.

She even got to skate with the
big snowman.
Best of all, she didn't fall once!

At last it was time to visit
the beautiful winter palace.

The whole thing was made of ice!
Lights inside made the palace glow.

"It really is a winter wonderland!"
said Ramona.
"Let's come back to Quebec City
next year!"